ABSOLUTE BEGIN...
Guide To Dr...

Crash Cymbal — Top-Tom

Cymbal Stand — Ride Cymbal

Hi-Hat Cymbals — Cymbal Stand

Snare Drum — Floor Tom

Hi-Hat Stand —

Bass Drum — Bass Drum Pedal

Snare Drum Stand —

Setting Up Your Kit

A basic kit comprises a bass (or 'kick') drum, snare, top tom-tom, floor tom, hi-hat stand, snare drum stand, bass drum pedal, two cymbal stands, one pair of hi-hat cymbals, one ride cymbal and one crash cymbal, as shown above.

When setting up your kit make sure everything is within easy reach. The height of your drum stool is important as this can affect the way you play. Go for a position where your legs are relaxed and in control of the pedals.

Tuning and the choice of drum heads can make a big difference to the overall sound of a drum. The tighter you tune a drum the higher its pitch will become. This also affects the speed of the stick response. The tighter the head the faster the response.

When tuning the snare drum try to have both heads quite tight with the snares just taut enough to stop them from rattling. If the snares are too tight it can stop them vibrating freely, causing them to sound choked.

Choose a head that is not too heavy as this can dull the sensitivity of the snares. I would suggest you try a Remo CS (centre spot) head for the batter (top) side and a Remo Ambassador Snare for the snare head (bottom side).

Tom-toms are not usually tuned to any specific notes but the smaller sizes are tuned to a higher pitch, getting lower as the sizes get larger. One thing to keep in mind when tuning the toms is to make sure they all have the same decay time (the time it takes for the sound to die away).

You can do this by playing one beat on each tom and listening to how long the note rings. Using a Zero Ring or a small piece of tissue paper (as damping) taped to the top head, positioned away from the area you are playing on, you can adjust the decay time.

More damping will result in a shorter decay, less damping will result in a longer decay.

Pull-Out Chart

The Bass Drum

The bass drum is generally tuned as low as possible without losing its tone. To achieve this tighten the heads only enough to take the wrinkles out. A pillow or blanket placed inside the drum against the back head is often used as damping to cut the ring down and produce a good solid thud.

There are two basic ways of playing the bass pedal. One way is to have the whole foot flat on the pedal, as shown in the first picture below. The other way is to raise the heel of your foot and only use your toes, as shown in the second picture.

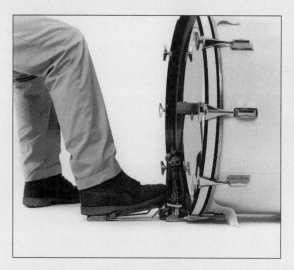 

Sometimes a combination of both methods is used. You might find using the toe method is easier for playing faster patterns. Try both ways to see which is the more comfortable for you.

When adjusting the tension spring on the bass pedal don't have it too tight or too loose. There should be just enough tension in the spring so that when you rest your foot on the pedal, the weight of your foot is enough to move the beater onto the head.

Bass drum beaters are usually made from felt or wood. A hard felt beater is the most commonly used as this produces a fast response and a good tone.

Care & Maintenance

Batter Head

Batter Counter Hoop

Nut Box

Tension Rod

Metal Shell

Snare Tension Screw

Snare Strainer Control Lever

Snare Counter Hoop

Snares

Snare Gate

Snare Head

A few points on general care and maintenance. A well maintained kit will last longer, look better and, more importantly, be less likely to let you down on a gig or recording session.

1) Keep all tension rods, screws, springs, snare release etc. lightly oiled.

2) As the snares are the most delicate part of the kit, try not to touch them unnecessarily and do not lay anything on top of them as this can cause the thin strands of wire to bend. If this happens the snares will vibrate unevenly causing an annoying buzz.

3) Cymbals can be cleaned (not too often) with a cymbal cleaner (obtained at most music stores) or washed with warm soapy water using a sponge, making sure you completely dry the cymbal after washing. Be careful not to use anything abrasive like metal cleaner or scouring pads as this can damage a cymbal. Do not clamp your cymbals to the stands too tightly as this can prevent them from vibrating freely and possibly cause them to crack.

4) Most drum heads are made of plastic and are very durable. However, with constant use they will gradually lose their tone and become less responsive and should be replaced.

To change a drum head, first unscrew (using a drum key) and remove all the tension rods, then lift off the counter hoop.

Remove the old head and fit the new one, replace the counter hoop and tension rods, then tune the head by tightening each tension rod in sequence (as shown in the diagram below) by one turn, until the required sound and feel are obtained.

5) Do not store your drums too near a heat source e.g. radiator, open fire etc.

6) When transporting your kit a set of waterproof fibre cases is recommended. These come in all different sizes so make sure you know the measurements of your drums before buying them.

Holding The Sticks

There are two basic ways of holding the sticks. One way is the matched grip, where both sticks are held in the same way.

The other is the traditional grip. Most rock drummers favour the matched grip (for power and speed) as shown below.

Matched Grip

Right hand: With the palm of your right hand facing towards the floor, hold the stick about one third of the distance from the butt end, so it pivots between the ball of the thumb and the joint of the first finger, as shown in the photograph.

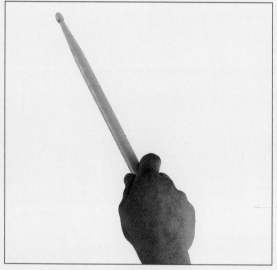

Let your first finger curl around the stick, then bring your second, third and fourth fingers gently around onto the stick to guide and stabilise it.

Left hand: The left hand grip should be exactly the same as the right hand. Try to keep both hands and fingers as relaxed as possible.

Say & Play *Book 1*

Drum*steps*

by **Geoff Battersby**

Wise Publications
London / New York / Paris / Sydney / Copenhagen / Madrid / Tokyo

Exclusive Distributors:
Music Sales Limited
14-15 Berners Street, London W1T 3LJ, UK.

Music Sales Corporation
257 Park Avenue South, New York, NY10010, USA.

Music Sales Pty Limited
20 Resolution Drive, Caringbah, NSW 2229, Australia.

Order No. AM 969518
ISBN 0-7119-8760-2
This book © Copyright 2001 by Geoff Battersby.
Published under exclusive licence by Wise Publications.

Written and arranged by Geoff Battersby.
CD recorded and produced by Kevin Wright.
Guitars by Kevin Wright and Paul Hale.

Cover & Book design by Phil Gambrill.
Music engraving by Paul Ewers Music Design.
Edited by Sorcha Armstrong.

Cover and text photographs by George Taylor.
Printed in the United Kingdom by
Printwise Ltd, Haverhill, Suffolk.

Geoff Battersby would like to give a special thanks to:
Bob Armstrong, Paul Francis, Stephen Chamberlain,
Malcolm Tabrett, Gwen Horlock, and to those who made
it possible to produce this book.

Your Guarantee of Quality:
As publishers, we strive to produce every
book to the highest commercial standards.
The music has been freshly engraved and the book
has been carefully designed to minimise awkward
page turns and to make playing from it a real pleasure.
Particular care has been given to specifying
acid-free, neutral-sized paper made from pulps which
have not been elemental chlorine bleached.
This pulp is from farmed sustainable forests and
was produced with special regard for the environment.
Throughout, the printing and binding have been
planned to ensure a sturdy, attractive publication
which should give years of enjoyment.
If your copy fails to meet our high standards,
please inform us and we will gladly replace it.

Contents

Introduction

Welcome to Drumsteps! You are now on your way to becoming a great player and reader on the drum kit. Think of becoming a great musician as a journey – so let's start that journey together as you take your first drumsteps in understanding and playing music on the drum kit.

I have had great fun playing and teaching drums throughout my career, performing in rock, jazz, blues and funk bands as a professional drummer. Having learnt to read drum music, I am also able to play in shows, musicals and big bands where reading drum notation is essential!

The *Say & Play* method will not only help you to master basic techniques, but will also help you to play in a range of styles and patterns. Starting with a brief look at music theory, the basics of the Drumsteps method – word association, and learning the rudiments, you'll then move on to playing whole 24-bar pieces, in five different styles – Funk, Shuffle, Jazz, Rock and Reggae, finishing off with a look at drum fills.

The accompanying CD demonstrates each musical example to help you hear what the rhythms should sound like, and also includes helpful 'click tracks' at different speeds, for you to practise with. The professionally recorded CD can be used time and time again to help you get it just right.

When you have learnt the material in this book, you will have opened up a whole new world, and will be able to gather new ideas from drum books and your favourite music magazines. Whether you're a would-be, or improving, drummer, this course will give you amazing results, in no time!

I hope you enjoy the book, and, most importantly, have fun with your drums. *Remember – if you can say it, you can play it!*

Geoff Battersby

Holding Your Sticks

By the time you've finished this section, you will have learnt five different note groups using the snare drum. You will then be able to continue through the examples in this book using the easy '*Say* & *Play*' method.

Sticking

Sticking is simply an indication of which sticks to use when playing on the snare drum. For these examples, please use alternate sticking. This means firstly use the right stick, then the left stick.

I have written this underneath the note groups, e.g. R L R L.

I'm left-handed!

No problem – simply reverse the sticking indications, and everytime you see R, play left, and likewise. For most examples, this will mean that you should start with the left stick, e.g. L R L R.

The Matched Grip

There are two main ways of holding the sticks. Most drummers use the **matched grip**, (shown below) which is what we'll be using here. It's important to find the most comfortable and efficient way of holding your sticks when you're playing. Try out both of these grips but I would recommend you stick to the **matched grip**, as it is the easiest.

Left stick on snare

Right stick on snare

Here's how to do it:

Hold the sticks between the first joint of your index finger and the fleshy part of your thumb in both hands, as pictured above, with the backs of the hands facing upwards.

Right hand grip

The Traditional grip

You can also hold your sticks in the **traditional grip** (below). Here's how to hold the traditional grip, for reference.

Left hand grip

Signs and Symbols

To get you started with reading drum notation, we've shown each symbol with a photo of the relevant drum above it.

Each drum has its own particular symbol or position within the stave (the lines on the page).

Don't worry if you can't remember all of these at once – we'll remind you later in the book. All you need to know to get started is the snare, hi-hat, and bass drum symbols. Think of pitch – the higher the sound, the higher it is on the stave, therefore the hi-hat is at the top, and the bass drum is at the bottom.

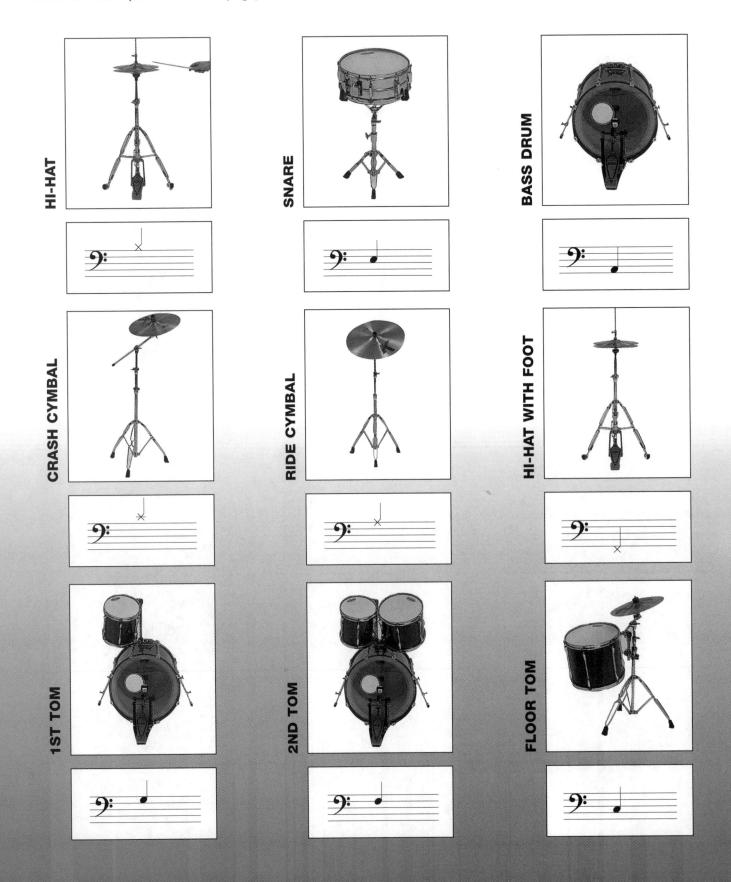

Music Theory

Have a look at the symbols below. These represent standard music notation and are helpful when trying to remember rhythms or play from a song sheet.

I have also added four 'dynamic' notations. Dynamics are best described as varying levels of volume from very loud to very soft. Although not used in this book, I feel it is important that you introduce them into your playing as soon as possible.

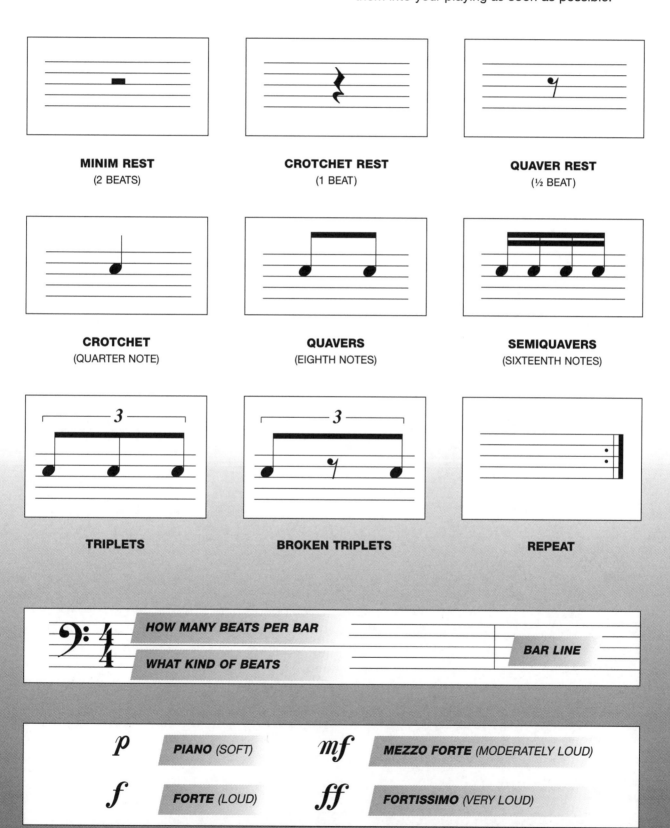

MINIM REST
(2 BEATS)

CROTCHET REST
(1 BEAT)

QUAVER REST
(½ BEAT)

CROTCHET
(QUARTER NOTE)

QUAVERS
(EIGHTH NOTES)

SEMIQUAVERS
(SIXTEENTH NOTES)

TRIPLETS

BROKEN TRIPLETS

REPEAT

HOW MANY BEATS PER BAR

WHAT KIND OF BEATS

BAR LINE

p   **PIANO** *(SOFT)*   *mf*   **MEZZO FORTE** *(MODERATELY LOUD)*

f   **FORTE** *(LOUD)*   *ff*   **FORTISSIMO** *(VERY LOUD)*

Posture and Grip

Here's how to sit at the drum kit. First, hold your sticks as previously shown.

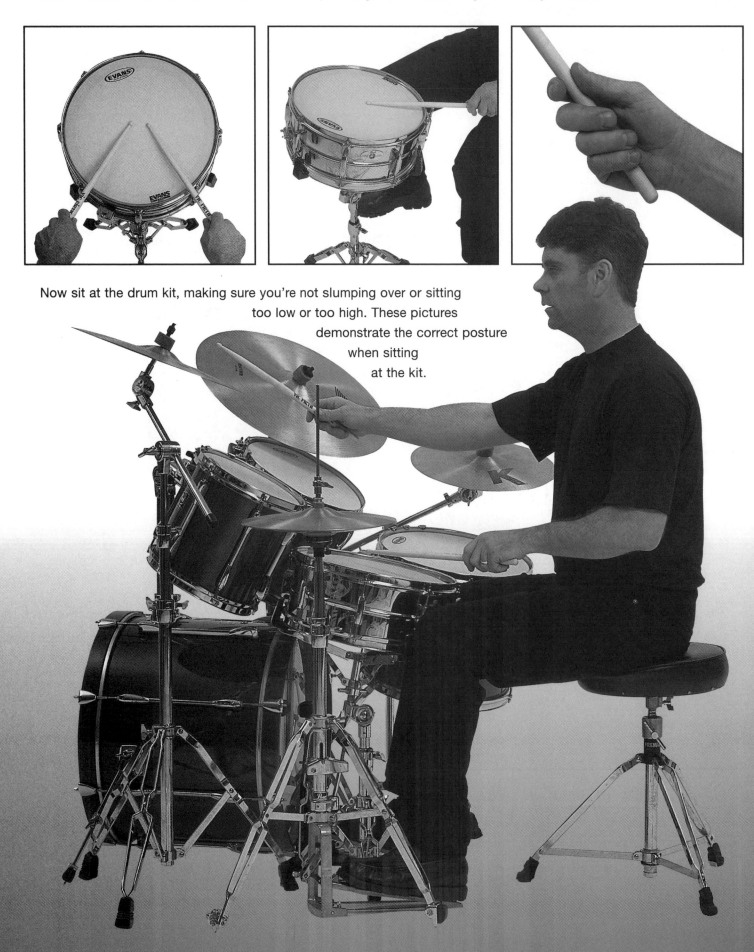

Now sit at the drum kit, making sure you're not slumping over or sitting too low or too high. These pictures demonstrate the correct posture when sitting at the kit.

Drumkit Layout

Here's how to set up your drum kit.

Most professional drummers carry a roll-up mat to gigs and sessions (pictured left) to save their drums from wear and tear, and to stop the bass drum slipping off the stage!

DRUMMING MAT

CRASH CYMBAL
400mm (16 inches)

1ST TOM TOM
250mm (10 inches)

RIDE CYMBAL
500mm (20 inches)

2ND TOM TOM
300mm (12 inches)

FLOOR TOM TOM
350mm (14 inches)

HI-HAT
350mm (14 inches)

SNARE DRUM
350mm (14 inches)

BASS DRUM
550mm (22 inches)

Your First Drumsteps

Now it's time to do some playing! Simply listen to the CD, repeat the word groups, and you'll be playing this in no time!

Remember, all examples on this page are played on the **snare** drum only. You'll need to use both sticks, alternating from left to right as indicated.

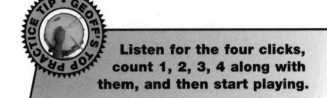

Listen for the four clicks, count 1, 2, 3, 4 along with them, and then start playing.

1-Beat Snare Rhythms

Snare Drum Rhythms

Once again, say and play each line on the snare drum using right / left sticking.

Listen carefully to the CD before playing, to hear how they should sound. All examples are preceded by 1 bar of clicks (4 clicks).

② 4-Beat Snare Rhythms

Even Rhythms

In this section, you will learn to read and play the first three British drum rudiments (sticking patterns) on the snare drum.

These are: **the single stroke roll**, **the double stroke roll** and **the single paradiddle**.

We'll then move on to some basic rock rhythms, using quarter notes, eighth notes and sixteenth notes. You'll be using these four-bar sections in the play along tracks later in the book.

TIME OUT!

Before you move on, here's what you already know. You can now:

- **Set up your drums**
- **Sit correctly at the drum kit**
- **Hold the sticks using the matched grip**
- **Read and understand the symbols for the hi-hat, snare and bass drum**
- **Play basic 1-bar rock rhythms**

It's much better to practise a little every day than a large amount once a week.

Here's a quick reminder of the drums you'll be using in this section, and their relevant symbols:

HI-HAT

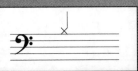

SNARE

BASS DRUM

Rudiments

Here are the basic three rudiments.
Listen to the CD, play them through once,
then practise them on your own.

Pay close attention to the sticking patterns, and
if necessary, practise them slowly first.

The little symbol at the end of each example is
called a **repeat** sign. This simply means that you
should repeat everything in that bar as many times
as indicated. If there is no indication, it means
repeat once.

For these examples, you should repeat once,
then twice, and then finally four times, in order to
build up your playing, although each example is
played only once on the CD.

The rudiments on this page are all played on the
snare drum.

GEOFF'S TOP PRACTICE TIP

You can practise your
rudiments at any time
using the click tracks on the
CD (Tracks 68-73). It's quite a good
warm-up before you start playing!

(3) The Single Stroke Roll

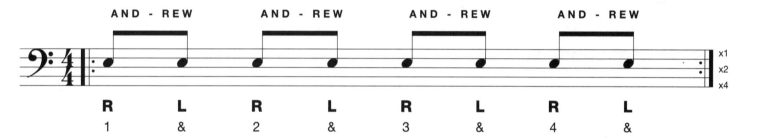

(4) The Double Stroke Roll

(5) The Single Paradiddle

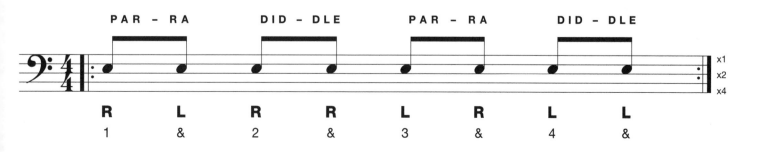

Quarter Note Rhythms

Say & **Play** this page to create a quarter note rhythm in 4/4 time.

You're now going to add in the hi-hat and the bass drum. Use your right hand to play the hi-hat, and your left to play the snare. Getting everything co-ordinated can be tricky at first, so take your time and start slowly!

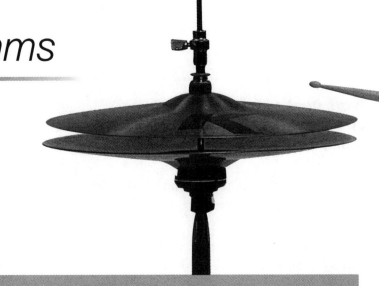

Remember, think of pitch when reading these rhythms. The hi-hat is at the top, the snare drum in the middle,

and the bass drum at the bottom of the stave – just the same as on your drum kit!

6 Hi-Hat Rhythm

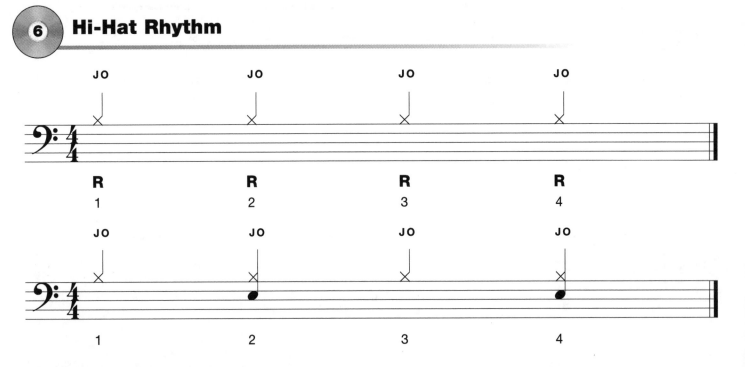

Now play this example once, adding the bass drum, and then four times with the guitar.

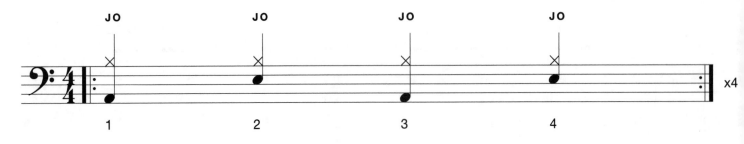

4-Bar Quarter Note Rock Rhythms

Say & **Play** this page to learn four very useful quarter note rhythms.

These four rhythms are great for developing hand/feet independence and co-ordination.

Be careful when you're playing the '&' beats – don't play hi-hat with the bass drum!

GEOFF'S TOP PRACTICE TIP

7 Quarter Note Rock 1

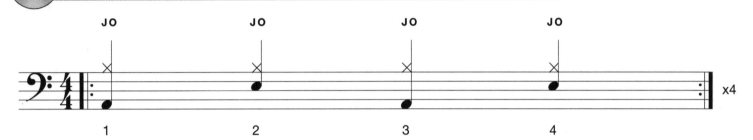

8 Quarter Note Rock 2

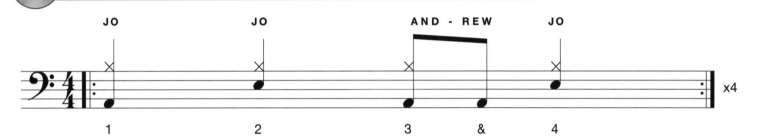

9 Quarter Note Rock 3

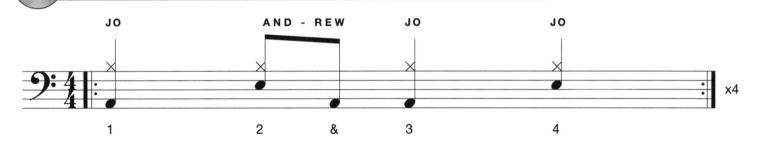

10 Quarter Note Rock 4

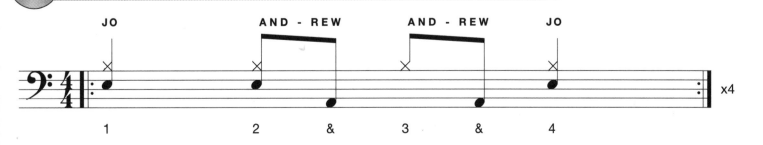

Eighth Note Rhythms

Say & **Play** this page to create an eighth note rhythm in 4/4 time.

This rhythm will allow you to play along to CDs of your favourite bands. Drummers such as **Steve White** (Paul Weller) & **Chad Smith** (Red Hot Chili Peppers) probably started out this way!

Count 'And-rew' along with the CD, practise the hi-hat rhythm, and then slowly add in the other drums.

Don't try to do it all at once! It's best to start slow, then speed up.

🄼 Eighth Note Hi-Hat Rhythm

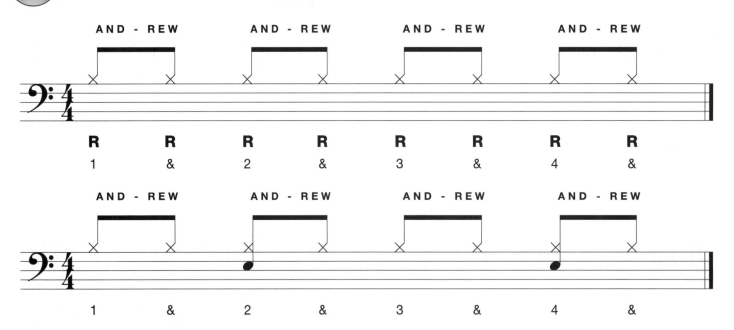

Now play this example once, adding the bass drum, and then four times with the guitar.

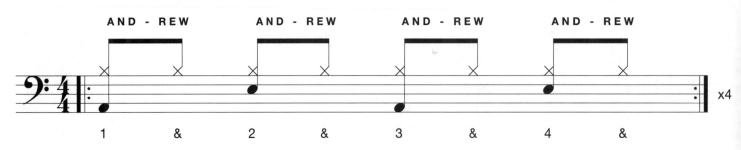

4-Bar Eighth Note Rock Rhythms

Learn each line separately, then play along to the CD tracks. Remember to play each line four times.

Here are four basic drum patterns for you to learn.

These can be used for practically any popular song. *Say* & *Play* this page along with the CD tracks to develop these important rhythms.

12 Eighth Note Rock 1

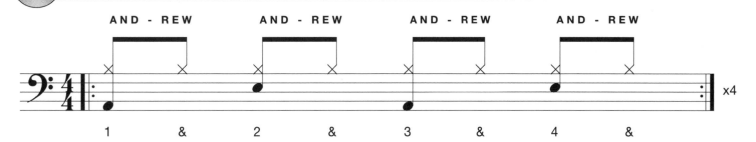

13 Eighth Note Rock 2

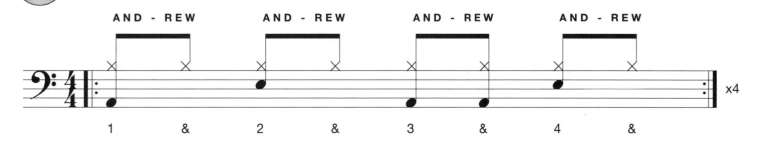

14 Eighth Note Rock 3

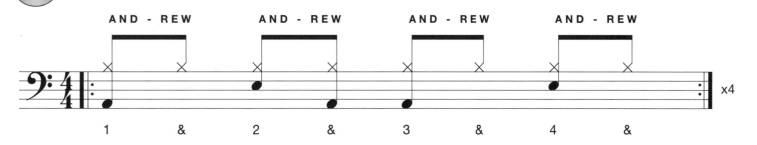

15 Eighth Note Rock 4

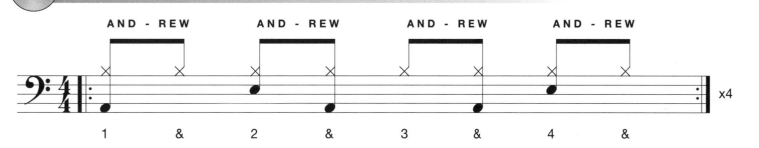

16th Note Rhythms

**Now we're moving on to some more
complicated rhythms – but still using
just three drums – the hi-hat, snare and
bass drum.**

On these two pages, you're playing sixteenth notes
(or semi-quavers) on the hi-hat – very quick notes.

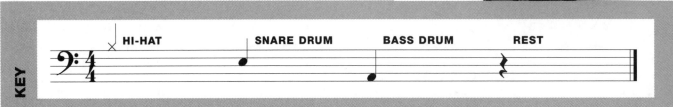

You'll find that this starts to 'drive' the rhythms more.
As before, **Say** & **Play** this page, making sure you're

confident with the new rhythms, then move on to
the longer examples on page 19.

16 16th Note Hi-Hat Rhythm

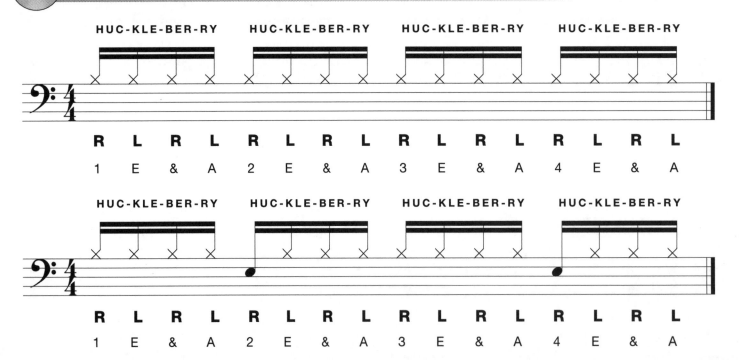

Now play this example once, adding the bass drum, and then four times with the guitar.

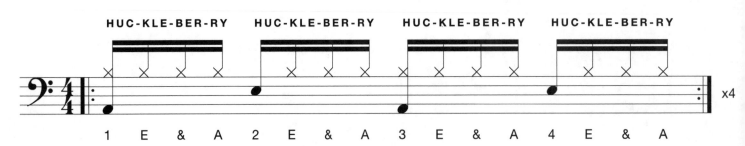

4-Bar 16th Note Rock Rhythms

In these rhythms the snare drum is played with the RIGHT stick.

(If you're left-handed, play the snare with the LEFT stick.)

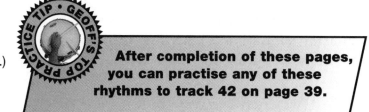

After completion of these pages, you can practise any of these rhythms to track 42 on page 39.

17 16th Note Rock 1

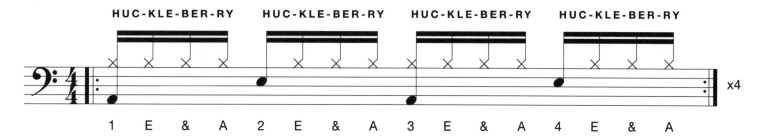

18 16th Note Rock 2

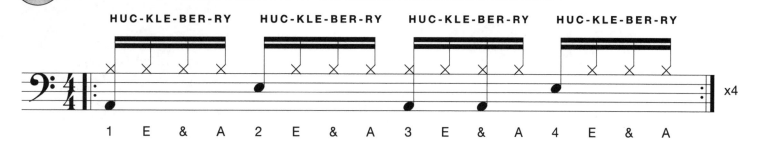

19 16th Note Rock 3

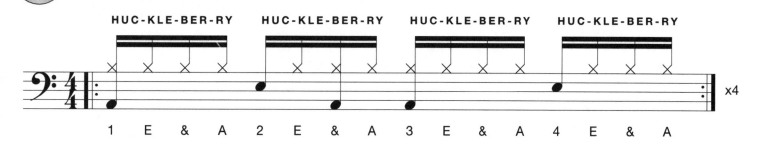

20 16th Note Rock 4

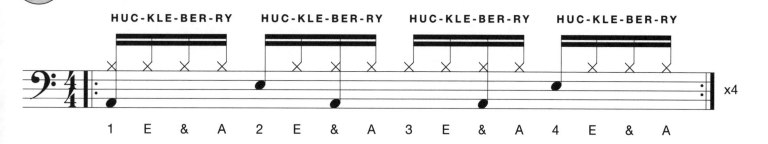

Styles

Now it's time to learn some new rhythms. We've already learnt how to play basic quarter note, eighth note and 16th note rhythms in a standard 'rock' style.

So let's move on and learn how to play shuffle, jazz, funk, and reggae. Once you've completed this section, you will be able to read and play five very useful rhythms.

If in doubt keep it simple – add the frills later.

TIME OUT!

Before you move on, here's what you already know. You can now:

• **Play the three basic rudiments – the single stroke roll, double stroke roll and the single paradiddle**

• **Play quarter note, eighth note and 16th note rhythms using the hi-hat, snare and bass drum**

Triplet Based Rhythms

Say *&* ***Play*** **these examples on the snare drum, using left / right sticking, to learn the basics of the 'swing' jazz sound.**

In this example, you're going to play eighth note triplets. Use the rhythm of the name Jo-an-na to help you.

The rhythms on this page are called 'triplets', which basically means squeezing three eighth notes into the space of two.

21 Triplet Rhythm 1

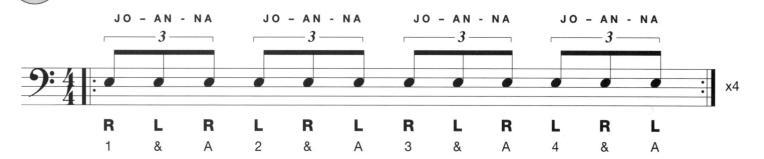

This time you're playing broken eighth note triplets, so instead of playing 'Jo-an-na', you miss out the middle

beat, and just play 'Jo-na'. Say the word Jo-an-na to yourself, but just play on the syllables Jo - Na.

22 Triplet Rhythm 2

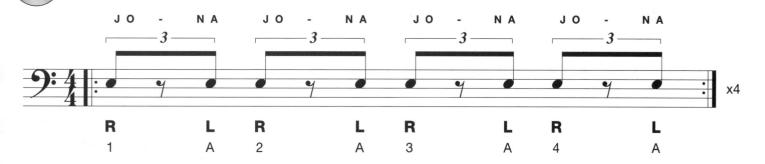

Now you're going to learn a jazz swing rhythm by playing a quarter note followed by broken triplets.

It's not as complicated as it looks! You're just putting together rhythms that you already know how to play. Use the rhythm of the words Jo, Jo-na to help you.

23 Triplet Rhythm 3

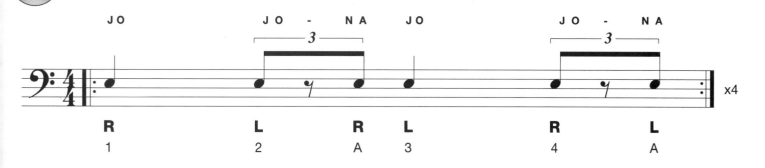

Preparation

Now we're altering the triplet rhythm slightly to create some new rhythms.

Say & **Play** the following rhythms using the right stick on the hi-hat or ride cymbal.

24 Shuffle

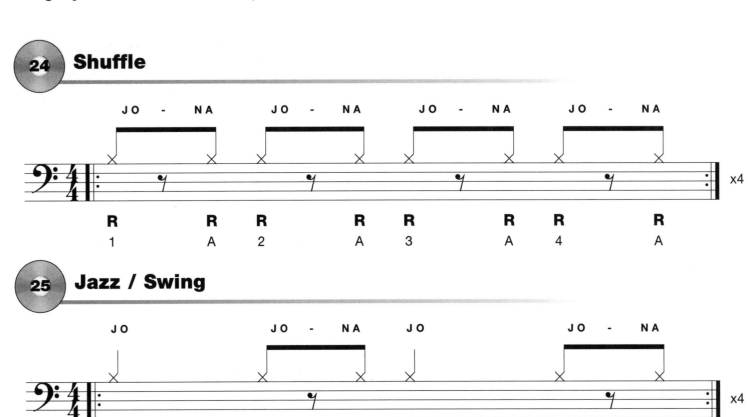

25 Jazz / Swing

26 Funk

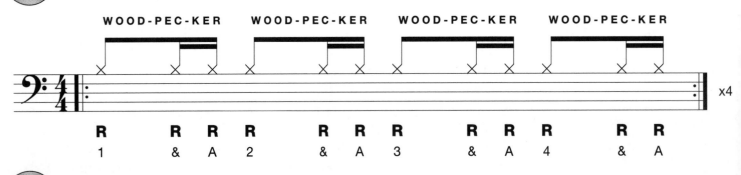

27 Reggae

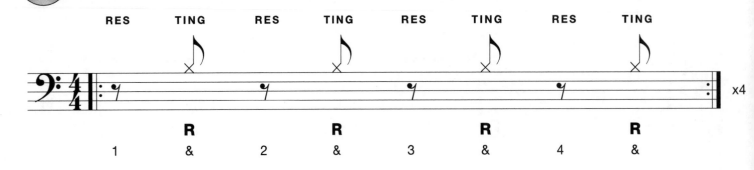

Shuffle Rhythm

This page is designed to teach you the basics of 'shuffle' – the R&B sound of artists like B.B. King or Eric Clapton.

You're using triplets on the hi-hat or ride cymbal, and straight beats on the snare and bass drum.

GEOFF'S TOP PRACTICE TIP

'Shuffle' usually means that the rhythm uses triplets, and is usually indicated above the music stave like this: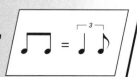

28 Jo-na Shuffle

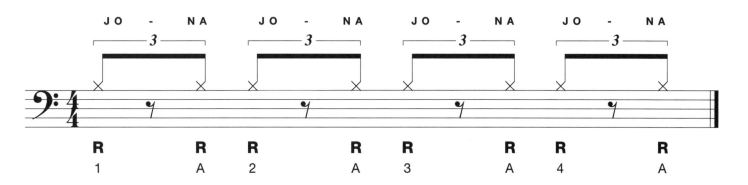

Now add the snare on the 2nd and 4th beats.

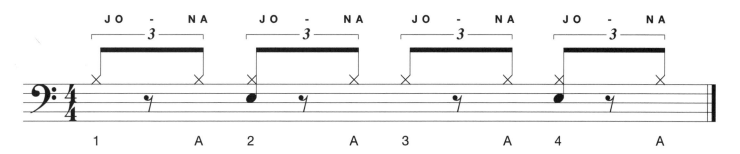

Finally, play this example once adding the bass drum, and then four times with the guitar.

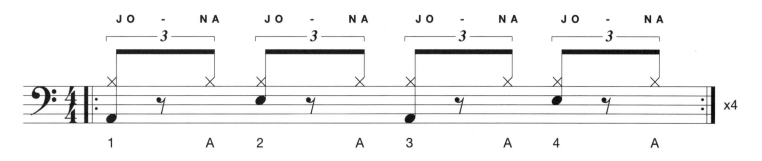

Jazz / Swing Rhythm

Even though it also uses triplet eighth notes, you'll find a subtle difference between this rhythm and the shuffle. It feels more laid-back.

Most of the rhythm comes from the hi-hat or ride cymbal (the top line of music), which makes the beat 'swing'. *Say* & *Play* this page to create a Jazz swing rhythm in 4/4 time.

29 Jo Jo-na Jazz

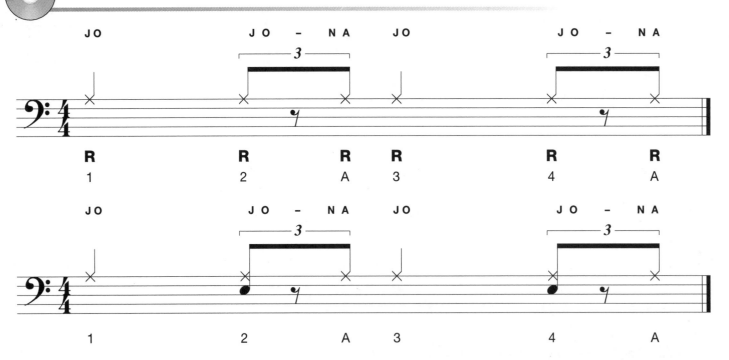

Now play this example once, adding the bass drum, and then four times with the guitar. The notes in

brackets are optional (play hi-hat with your foot).

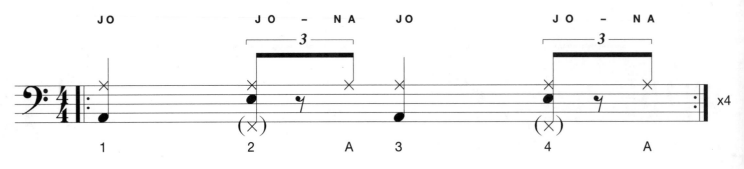

Funk Rhythm

Once you've completed this page, you'll be able to play a funk rhythm in 4/4 time.

Say & *Play* the examples below, adding snare and then bass drum to the hi-hat. Make sure you're not still playing in triplets!

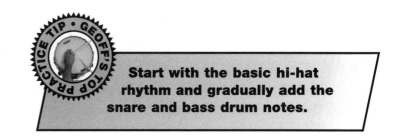

Start with the basic hi-hat rhythm and gradually add the snare and bass drum notes.

30 **Wood-pec-ker Funk**

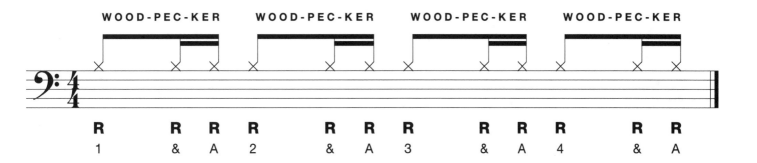

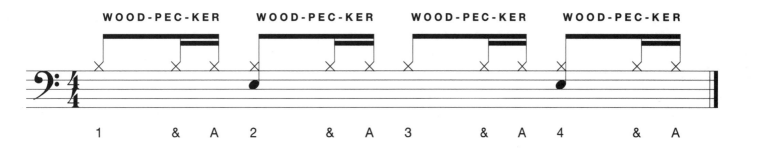

Finally, play this example once adding the bass drum, and then four times with the guitar.

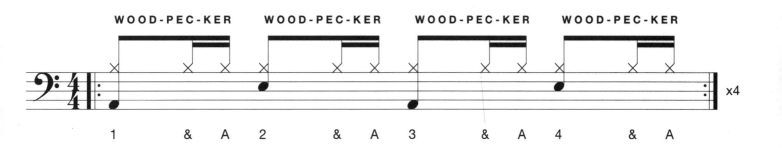

Reggae Rhythm

Say & **Play** this page to create eighth note reggae rhythms using the hi-hat, snare and bass drum.

You've already played the hi-hat part for this reggae rhythm, on page 22. Make sure that you play only on the off-beats (on the '&').

31 Res-ting Reggae

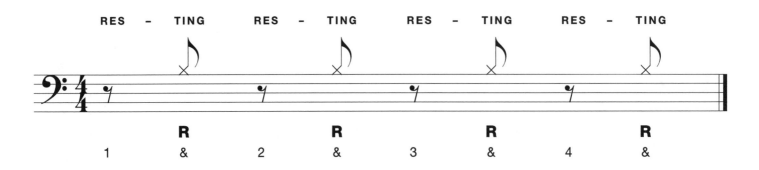

Now add the snare drum, making sure not to play the hi-hat with it. This is a fairly simple rhythm, so it's important to stay in time and not to speed up or slow down.

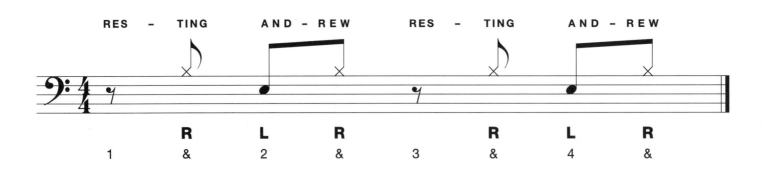

Finally, play this example once adding the bass drum, and then four times with the guitar.

For some reggae influences, listen to **Bob Marley and the Wailers**, and British bands like **UB40** and **The Police**.

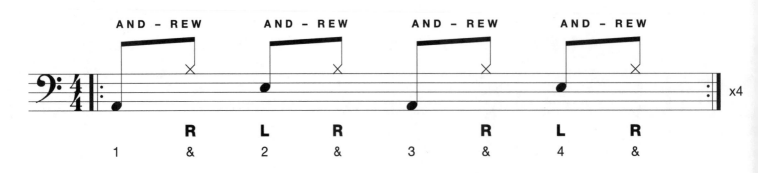

The Four Basic Rock Grooves

If you've completed the last section and feel confident with all the rhythms you've just learned – congratulations!

You're another step closer to becoming a competent drummer. Now you need to build on what you've just learned, by lengthening and altering the basic beats.

When you have completed this section, you will be able to play four basic rock rhythms in a 24-bar format, along with guitar and bass accompaniment. The rhythms change in the middle section (the 'middle 8'), usually meaning that you have to use the ride cymbal instead of the hi-hat. You'll also be using the crash cymbal to mark the start of every four-bar phrase.

You will also learn about song structure, as most modern rock & pop music is made up of 4, 8, 12,

16, or 24-bar phrases. Although this is a 24-bar piece, the phrases are only 4 bars long (each time you hit the crash cymbal you're starting a new phrase).

GEOFF'S TOP PRACTICE TIP

Listen to as much music as possible and find drummers or bands whose style you like. Most famous musicians name-check their influences at one time or another, so it's a good idea to have some to hand!

Take a moment now to remind yourself of the different symbols on the drum notation that you'll be using in this section. The symbols for hi-hat, crash cymbal and ride cymbal are very similar, so you might want to make a note of these separately so that you can easily refer to them while you're playing.

TIME OUT!

Before you move on, here's what you already know.

You can now:

- **Use triplet-based rhythms**
- **Read and understand rests**
- **Play basic shuffle, jazz, funk, reggae and rock rhythms using hi-hat, snare and bass drum**

HI-HAT

SNARE

RIDE CYMBAL

BASS DRUM

Basic Quarter Note Rock Groove

Here's your first 24-bar rock rhythm.

You'll find that you already know this rhythm, from earlier in the book – but we've made it longer and added some changes. Listen to the CD and then have a go yourself!

32

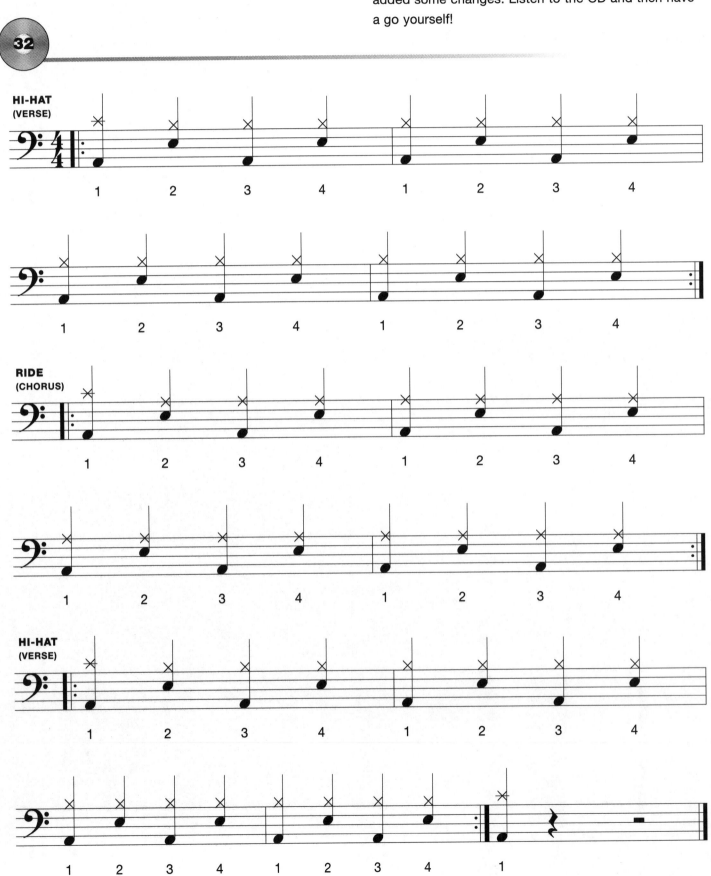

24-bar Rock Groove 1

Say & Play this page to develop good timekeeping.

Play 8 bars on the hi-hat, 8 bars on the ride cymbal, then 8 bars on the hi-hat again. Use the crash cymbal to mark the start of each 4 bar phrase.

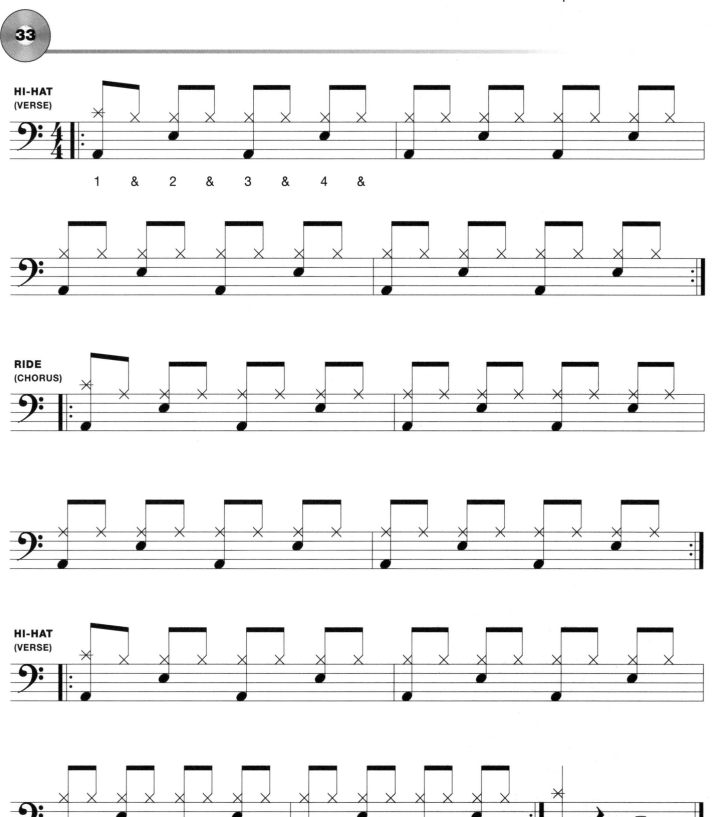

24-bar Rock Groove 2

**Now we're going to break up the snare
and bass drum lines, while keeping the
eighth note hi-hat rhythm going.**

Why not listen to your favourite music and see
if you can find a song that uses this rhythm.

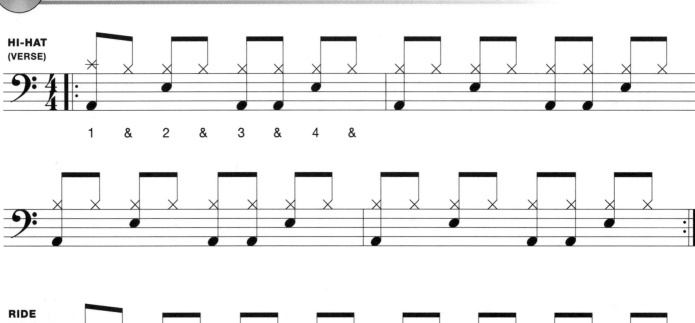

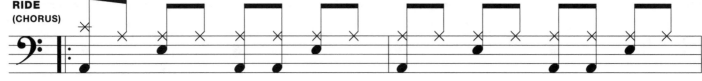

24-bar Rock Groove 3

Play 24 bars with guitar and bass. Warning! Rock Groove 2 and Rock Groove 3 are similar, but not the same.

When you are comfortable playing these pieces you can look at the drum fills section with a view to adding them to Rock Grooves 1-4.

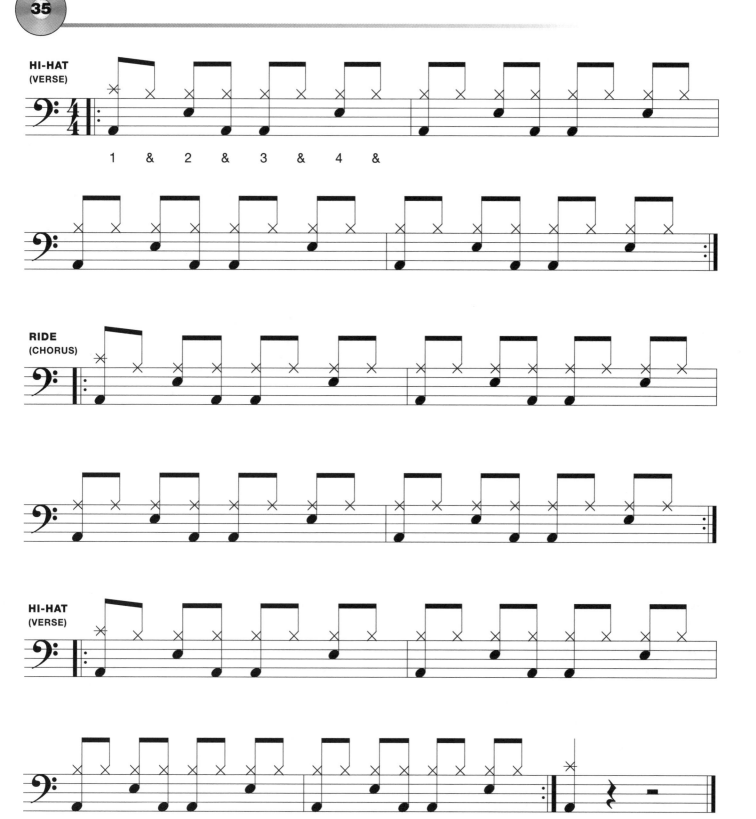

24-bar Rock Groove 4

**This is the most demanding of all the
rock rhythms that you've played so far,
so be careful with your co-ordination.**

Why not practise it really slowly first – and listen
to the CD as well, before trying it on your own?

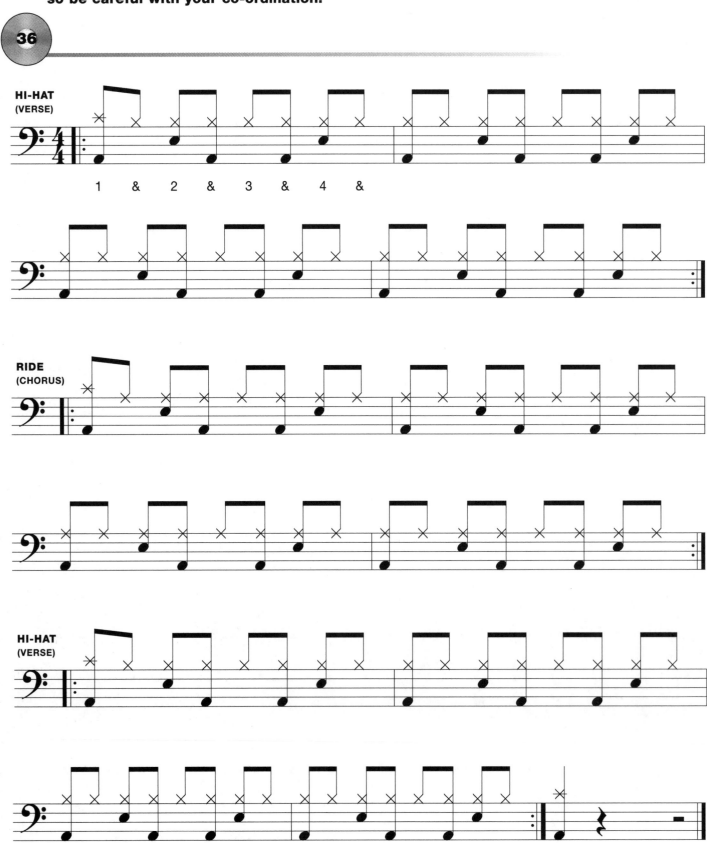

Play Along Tracks

When you have completed this section
you will be able to play a selection of
24-bar tracks using the five different styles
you've already looked at, with guitar and
bass accompaniment.

There are five different styles, all in the
24-bar format, followed by another 24-bar
Rock piece using sixteenth notes.
As before, use the crash cymbal to mark
the start of each four bar phrase.

When you're comfortable with the structure of
these pieces, you can add one beat fills to the end
of each 4 bar phrase, and two beat fills to the
end of the 8 bar phrase. There's more about
fills in the next section.

Here's another quick reminder of the symbols
you'll be reading, although you should be
getting more familiar with them now.

GEOFF'S TOP PRACTICE TIP

You can use the click tracks on
the CD (tracks 68-73) to
practise any of the material you've
learned so far (see page 47).

TIME OUT!

Before you move on, here's what you already know.
You can now:

- **Play 24 bars of 4 basic rock rhythms**
- **Use the crash and ride cymbals and
  understand the different notation symbols**
- **Understand song structure**

HI-HAT

SNARE

RIDE CYMBAL

BASS DRUM

Rock Solid

Before we move on to the play along tracks, let's try speeding up Rock 1 – the first basic rock rhythm you learned.

Play 24 bars with guitar and bass, as before, with a crash cymbal marking every 4 bar phrase, and a middle eight section using the ride cymbal.

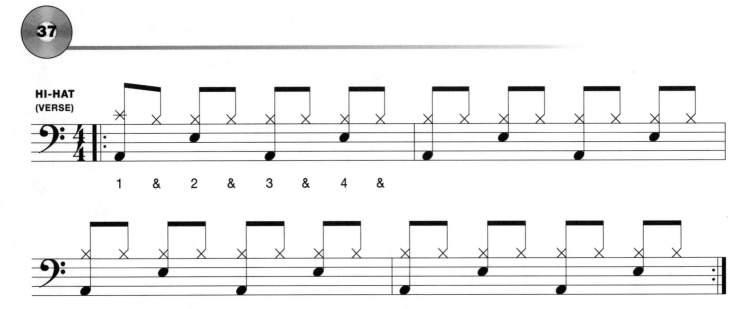

HI-HAT
(VERSE)

1   &   2   &   3   &   4   &

RIDE
(CHORUS)

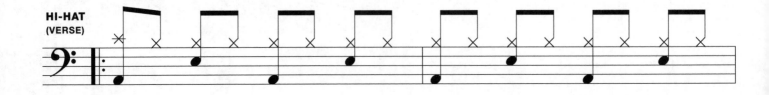

HI-HAT
(VERSE)

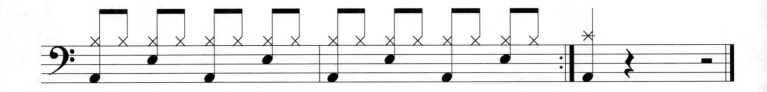

Shuffle and Swing

Now you have a chance to play 24 bars of the shuffle rhythm – plenty of practise for those 'swung' quavers (broken triplets).

Be careful not to slip into Rock 1 when playing the shuffle.

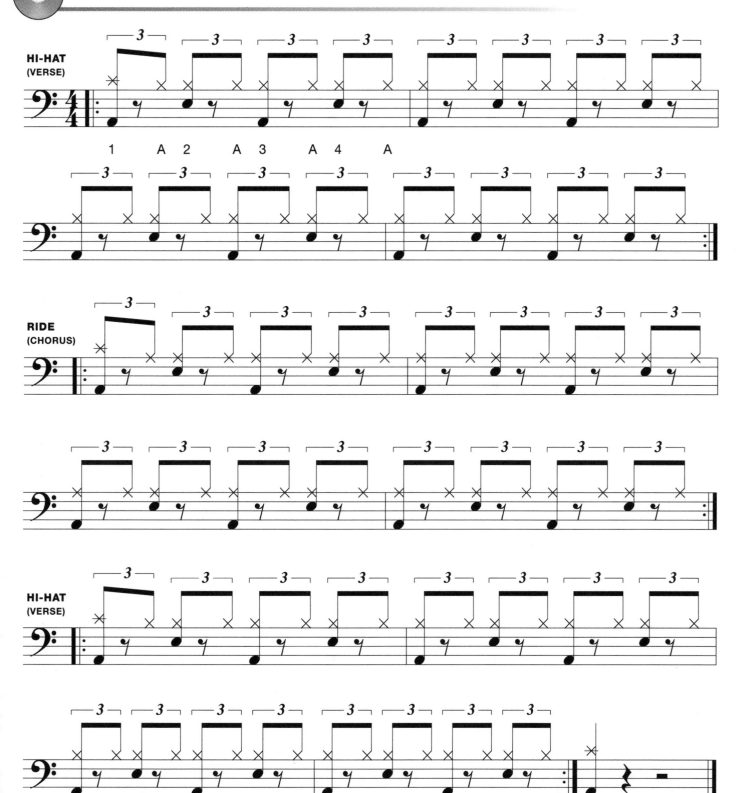

Jo Jo-Na Jazz

Learn this 24 bar Jazz piece and become The King of Swingers! Try out the hi-hat first, to get you into the 'swing' of this piece.

You're also playing the hi-hat with your foot in this piece, so be careful you don't hit the bass drum instead! Getting the co-ordination right will be your biggest challenge for this piece.

39

Feeling Funky

It's time to get funky! This features a faster, more upbeat hi-hat rhythm, but be very careful not to lapse back into swung triplets.

Remember to say 'wood-peck-er' each time you play the hi-hat.

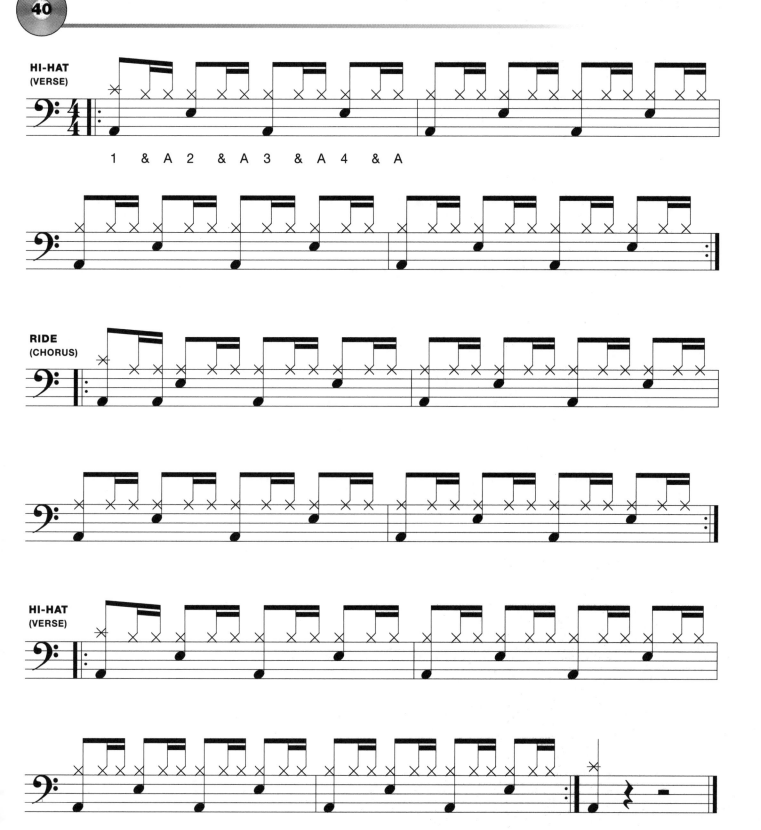

1 & A 2 & A 3 & A 4 & A

Rest - Ting Reggae

24 bars of laid-back reggae beats – just make sure you don't get so laid-back you fall off your stool!

Use bass or snare when you say Rest, and Hi-hat with the right stick when you say Ting.

Super Sixteenths

This piece gives you a chance to practise using even faster hi-hat notes, but they're evenly spaced.

Watch out for the alternating ride cymbal/ hi-hat rhythm in the middle 8!

42

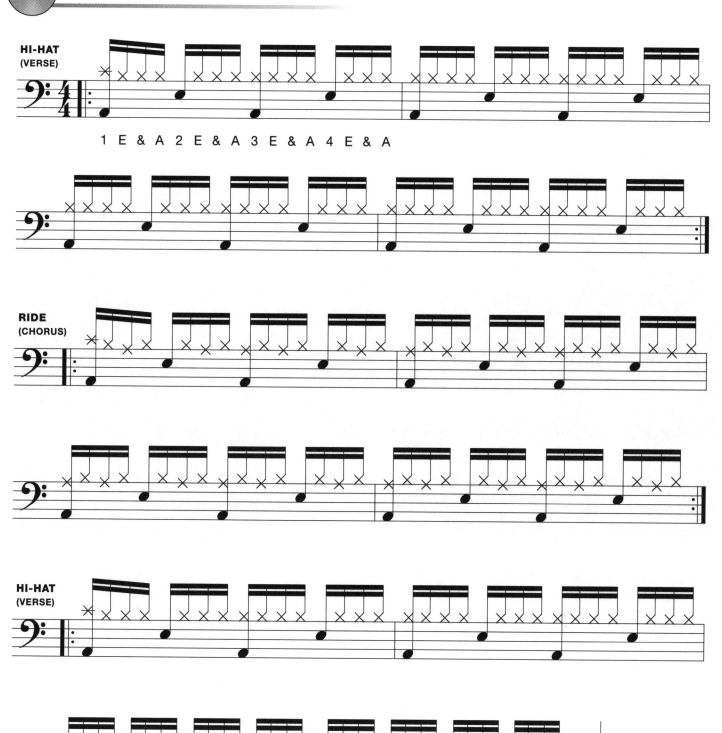

1 E & A 2 E & A 3 E & A 4 E & A

Drum Fills

Now it's time to put the finishing touches to your 24-bar rhythms, by adding drum fills.

Drum fills can be used at the beginning or the end of a song, and also to begin or end musical phrases. Think of them as musical commas or full stops.

When you are comfortable with playing the pieces in the book, gradually add the drum fills. The fills on the next few pages will be played on the toms and snare – so take a moment to remind yourself of the different notation (see page 6).

Use R/L sticking when playing tracks 43-47, then you may prefer to lead with the right stick or the left stick for left handed players.

Please use alternate sticking where possible (right/left), but in some cases you may need to change the sticking. I have found that Wood-peck-er works better played R-RL, or L-LR for left handed players.

TIME OUT!

Before you move on, here's what you already know. You can now:

- **Play 24 bars of drum rhythm in five different styles**
- **Play the hi-hat with your foot, along with other complicated rhythms**
- **Read and understand drum notation, song structure and other markings (repeat signs, etc).**

Basic Drum Fills

Let's use the word association method to help learn and play these rhythms on the snare drum & tom toms.

43 Quarter Note Fill

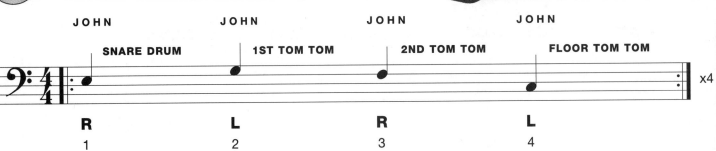

Basic Drum Fills (Continued)

44 Eighth Note Fill

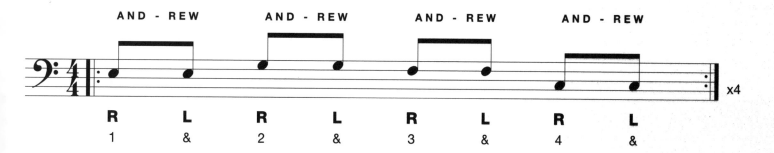

45 16th Note Fill

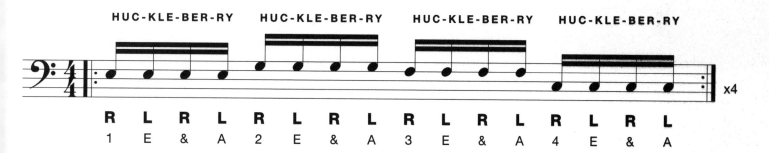

46 Lem-on-ade Fill

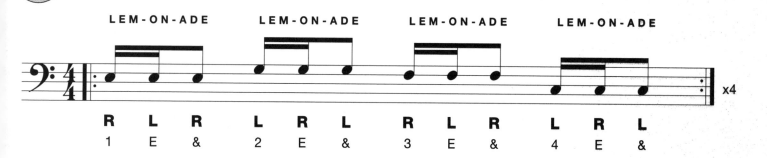

47 Wood-pec-ker

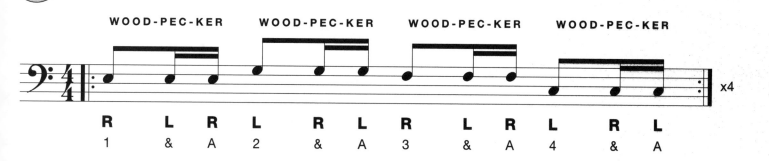

One Beat Drum Fills

Now let's try some shorter fills – a bar of rhythm, with a one-beat fill.

Use these fills to act as a musical comma or full stop in the music.

48 And-rew Fill

49 Huc-kle-ber-ry Fill

50 Lem-on-ade Fill

51 Wood-pec-ker Fill

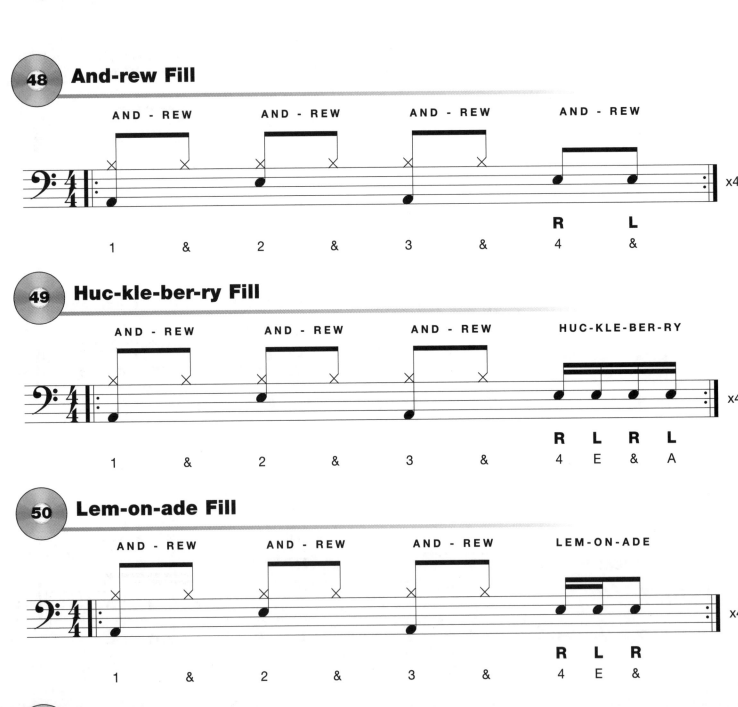

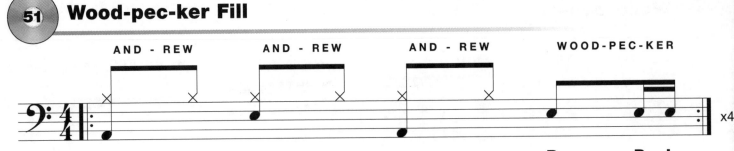

Two Beat Drum Fills

Use R/L sticking or right hand lead,
left handers use left hand lead.

Practice these fills as written,
then play the crash cymbal on
beat 1, instead of the hi-hat.

52 **And-rew Fill 2**

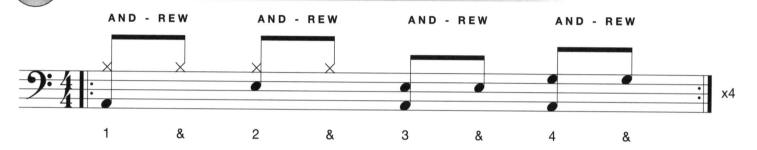

53 **Huc-kle-ber-ry Fill 2**

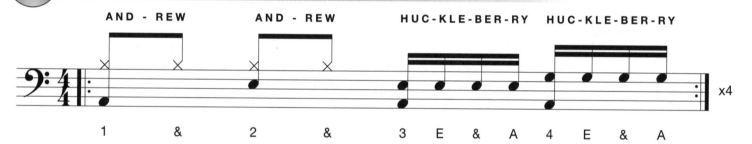

54 **Lem-on-ade Fill 2**

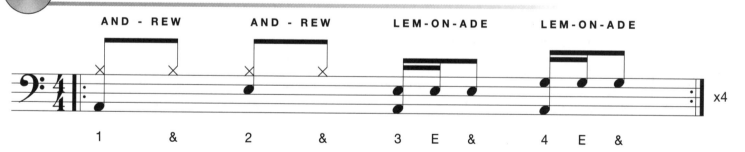

55 **Wood-pec-ker Fill 2**

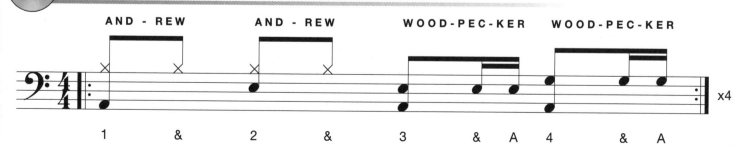

One Bar Drum Fills

Play one bar of time adding the crash cymbal to beat 1, then play a one-bar drum fill.

When you're using these fills in longer pieces, remember to mix them up a bit – don't always use the same ones. Experiment yourself with some new rhythms. Play the bass drum on all four beats of the drum fill.

56 And-rew Fill 3

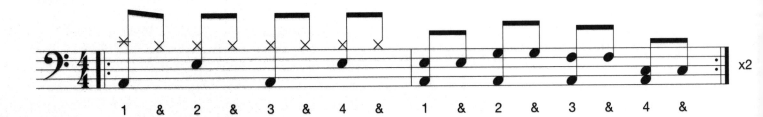

57 Huc-kle-ber-ry Fill 3

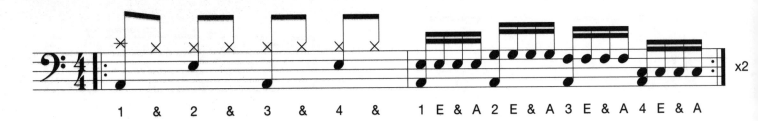

58 Lem-on-ade Fill 3

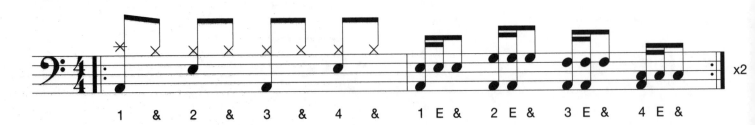

59 Wood-pec-ker Fill 3

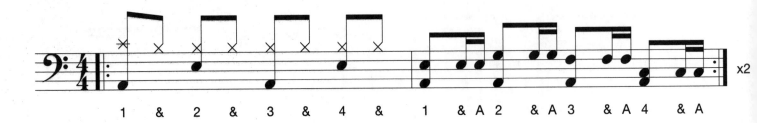

One Bar Triplet Fills

Each of these fills is repeated four times, to give you more time to practise.

When playing these triplets, use R/L sticking. You will notice that each triplet group starts with R then L stick, the reverse for left handers.

60 Jo-an-na Fill

61 Jo-an-na Fill 2

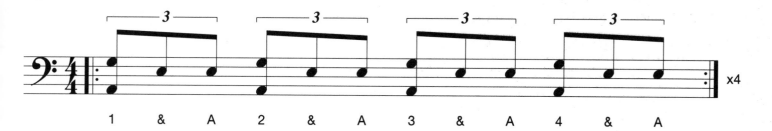

62 Jo-an-na Fill 3

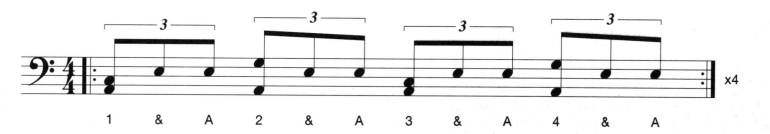

63 Jo-an-na Fill 4

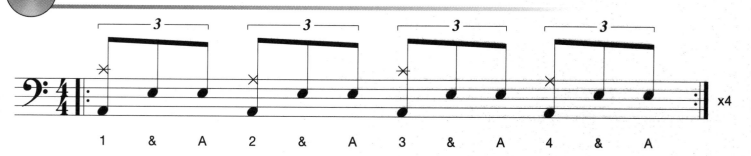

One Bar Triplet Fills

Now let's mix it up a bit...

Don't worry – it's not as complicated as it looks! Just take it slowly to start with, and then build up speed.

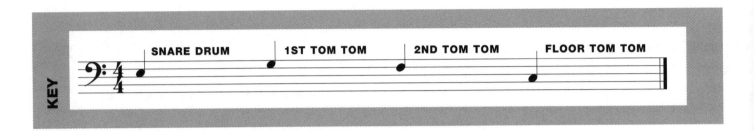

64 **2-bar Triplet Fill**

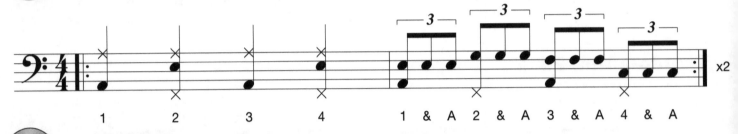

65 **2-bar Triplet Fill 2**

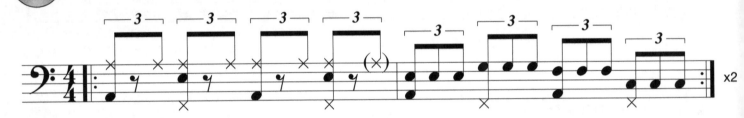

66 **2-bar Triplet Fill 3**

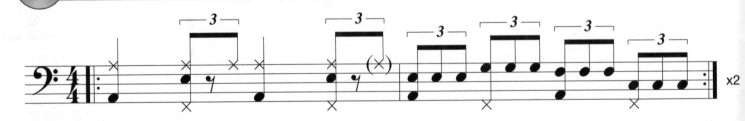

67 **2-bar Triplet Fill 4**

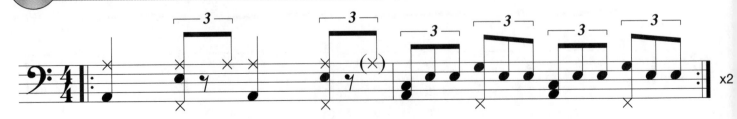

Please note that the ride cymbals in brackets (X) are optional.

Click Tracks

Practising with a metronome is widely agreed to be one of the best ways to help you stay in time. As a drummer, it's essential to play in time, for the rest of the band to follow you.

Soon, you'll develop your own sense of rhythm and will be able to play at any speed without speeding up or slowing down.

But if you don't have your own metronome, don't worry – we've recorded some handy click tracks for you, at six different speeds.

A metronome will provide you with a much wider range of beats and speeds, but these click tracks are a good starting point.

Use these to practise all the rhythms you've learned in this book, at slow and fast speeds. Each track is about 3 minutes long.

CLICK   CLICK   CLICK   CLICK

68 **40 Beats Per Minute**

69 **60 Beats Per Minute**

70 **80 Beats Per Minute**

71 **100 Beats Per Minute**

72 **110 Beats Per Minute**

73 **120 Beats Per Minute**

Further Reading

Congratulations! You've completed Book One of the Drumsteps method, and are now ready to move on to more advanced material.

Here are some other great books, available from all good music retailers or bookshops.

In case of difficulty, contact Music Sales directly (see p2 for details) or log on to www.musicsales.com.

Fast*forward* Rock Solid Drum Patterns
AM92666
Learn the essentials of rock rhythms, including bass and snare drum variations, drum fills, syncopated rhythms, and much more. For the beginner to intermediate player.

Chart Reading Workbook For Drummers
HLE00695129
Book and CD pack covers common symbols, musical shorthand, ensemble figures, set-up ideas and more.

Fast Track Drums Level 1
HLE00697285
Learn to play the drums the fast way. A collection of songs and examples, beats and fills, rock, blues and funk styles, syncopation, improvisation and much more.

Fast Track Drums Songbooks
The fast, fun way to learn the drums. The songbooks are compatible with other Fast Track songbooks, and feature eight songs so that bands can jam together.

Level 1 Songbook 1
HLE00695367
Includes 'Brown Eyed Girl', 'I Want To Hold Your Hand', 'Wild Thing', 'Wonderful Tonight' and 'You Really Got Me'.

Level 1 Songbook 2
HLE00697290
Includes ' Jailhouse Rock', 'Twist and Shout', 'Have I Told You Lately', 'Gimme Some Lovin' and 'Gloria'.

Remember to keep practising and playing along to your favourite tracks. See you in Book 2...

Say & Play **Book 2**

Drumsteps

The following examples are just a taste of what to expect from Book 2. You will learn more exciting *Say & Play* words and rudiments, rhythms, fills and styles.